20th Century

RACE TO THE MOON

Stephanie Paris

Consultants

Timothy Rasinski, Ph.D.
Kent State University

Lori Oczkus
Literacy Consultant

Matt Heverly
NASA Engineer

Based on writing from
TIME For Kids. TIME For Kids and the *TIME For Kids* logo are registered trademarks of TIME Inc. Used under license.

Publishing Credits

Dona Herweck Rice, *Editor-in-Chief*
Lee Aucoin, *Creative Director*
Jamey Acosta, *Senior Editor*
Lexa Hoang, *Designer*
Stephanie Reid, *Photo Editor*
Rane Anderson, *Contributing Author*
Rachelle Cracchiolo, *M.S.Ed., Publisher*

Image Credits: p.17 (top) Alamy; p10 (right) The Bridgeman Art Library; pp.8–9 Corbis; pp.4, 11 (right), 40, 50 Getty Images; pp. 6,19 (bottom) iStockphoto; pp.2–3, 4–5, 7(right), 10(middle), 12-13, 19 (top), 20, 28, 29 (top), 30–45, 48–49, 49, 54–61 NASA; p.44 NASA/U.S. Customs and Border Patrol; p.10 (left) Newscom; p.12 AFP/Newscom; pp.16, 59, akg-images/RIA Nowosti/Newscom; pp.11 (left), 18 ITAR-TASS/Newscom; p.21 REUTERS/Newscom; p.15 Rick Davis/Splash News/Newscom; pp.6–7, 10–11, 24, 28–29, 47(left), 50–51, 53–54 Photo Researchers Inc.; pp.14–15, 53 (illustrations) Kevin Panter; pp.43 (illustrations) Timothy J. Bradley; All other images from Shutterstock.

Teacher Created Materials

5301 Oceanus Drive
Huntington Beach, CA 92649-1030
http://www.tcmpub.com

ISBN 978-1-4333-4899-0

TABLE OF CONTENTS

Space Race 4

High Flying Heroes 16

To the Moon 30

What's Next?. 46

Glossary. 58

Index 60

Bibliography 62

More to Explore 63

About the Author 64

SPACE RACE

Today, most people have cell phones. **Satellite** television is common. Every science textbook has pictures of Earth from outer space. But just 60 years ago, none of these things were possible. In the 1950s, we couldn't send objects beyond Earth's atmosphere. Then, we sent humans into space. We even landed **astronauts** on the moon. This was a time of discovery and great accomplishments. It was also a lot of work. Scientists from around the world gathered in the United States and the **Soviet Union**. They struggled, failed, and learned. Some made the ultimate sacrifice. They gave their lives to the cause. But in the end, what they achieved remains awesome!

THINK LINK

- What was the **space race**?
- What difficulties did NASA face sending people to the moon?
- What does it take to be an astronaut?

COLD WAR, HOT TECHNOLOGY

During World War II, scientists made impressive **rockets**. The rockets were powerful enough to launch bombs into distant countries. But scientists wondered if they could be used for something else. Were they powerful enough to be fired into outer space? People have always been curious about what lies beyond Earth. At the end of the war, American and Soviet scientists began working toward this goal. But the two countries were enemies. And they didn't trust each other. This time period was called the **Cold War**. Instead of working together, each country began to compete. They both wanted to win the space race.

THE RACE

The space race between the United States and the **Union of Soviet Socialist Republics (USSR)** lasted from 1957 until 1969.

Sputnik 1, the first man-made satellite

SOVIETS

The Soviets were the people who lived in the USSR from 1917 to 1991. They formed a powerful political group.

MISSILES

During the Cold War, the USSR and the United States built thousands of nuclear **missiles**. Each country wanted to have stronger weapons than the other. They thought this would keep them safe from attack. The same technology used to launch missiles also sends rockets into space. It was a dangerous time. But each missile that was launched taught us more about how to explore space.

ASTRO-SPIES

During the Cold War, both countries used their space programs to spy on each other. It was a dangerous game. If a spy was caught, it meant prison, or worse—death. Check out some of the secret missions developed for the astronauts and their eyes in the sky.

- Capture or destroy a satellite.

- Determine the number of weapons and planes on the ground.

- Practice for battles in space.

- Launch a spy station into orbit, equipped with a car-size camera.

"What makes the Soviet threat unique in history is its all-inclusiveness. Every human activity is pressed into service as a weapon of expansion. Trade, economic development, military power, arts, science, education, the whole world of ideas....The Soviets are, in short, waging total cold war."

—President Dwight D. Eisenhower, 1958

a missile test launch

OCTOBER SURPRISE

On October 4, 1957, Soviet scientists had the first major success in the space race. They launched Sputnik 1. This was Earth's first artificial satellite. It was the first non-natural thing to orbit the planet. The United States was caught off guard. It was working on its own satellite. But it wasn't ready. Soon, Soviet scientists had a string of impressive firsts. The competition was heating up. And the United States was falling behind.

FAMOUS FIRSTS

First Dog in Space
Laika, November 3, 1957

First Man in Space
Yuri Gagarin, April 12, 196

First American Satellite
Explorer 1, January 31, 1958

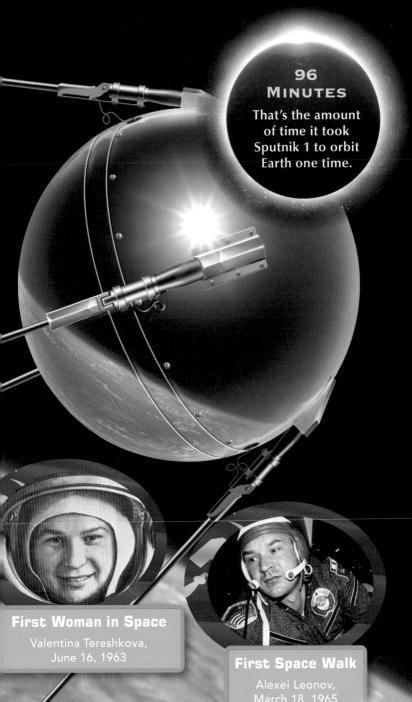

96 MINUTES

That's the amount of time it took Sputnik 1 to orbit Earth one time.

First Woman in Space

Valentina Tereshkova, June 16, 1963

First Space Walk

Alexei Leonov, March 18, 1965

THE KENNEDY CHALLENGE

"I believe that this nation should commit itself to achieving the goal, before this decade is out, of landing a man on the moon and returning him safely to the Earth." In 1961, President John F. Kennedy issued this challenge to Americans. He knew it would be hard. But he said, "No single space project will be more...impressive to mankind." Setting a goal can help people manage their time. It can motivate them. And it can make them push themselves harder. The Apollo program was designed to make Kennedy's idea real.

TEAMWORK LOST

President Kennedy wanted to find a way for American and Soviet scientists to work together. He thought it would be easier to get to the moon if everyone shared information. But on November 22, 1963, President Kennedy was **assassinated**. His dreams of the United States and the Soviet Union working together were put on hold for another 30 years.

By the time the Americans landed on the moon, the Apollo Program cost $24 billion.

WHAT'S IN A NAME?

The American space program was named after the ancient Greek god Apollo. He was believed to be the god of the sun, pulling it across the sky each day.

KENNEDY SPACE CENTER

President Kennedy made getting into space a national priority. That's one reason the space center in Florida is named after him. Since 1968, the National Aeronautics and Space Administration (NASA) has launched most missions from the Kennedy Space Center. If you are nearby, you can take a tour of it. What would you want to see first?

Rocket Garden

Tour the rocket garden to compare the first rockets that put NASA astronauts in space.

Space Shop

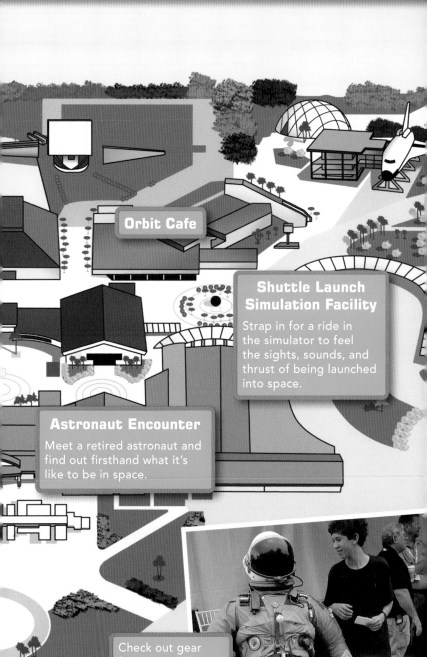

Orbit Cafe

Shuttle Launch Simulation Facility

Strap in for a ride in the simulator to feel the sights, sounds, and thrust of being launched into space.

Astronaut Encounter

Meet a retired astronaut and find out firsthand what it's like to be in space.

Check out gear from past missions.

HIGH FLYING HEROES

Getting to space is not something one person can do alone. Thousands of people worked on the space programs. Some traveled into space. Others worked on Earth to design the shuttles. They looked for the safest way to explore the solar system. The USSR and the United States both needed engineers to design the space ships. And they needed pilots to fly them. In the United States, these space travelers were called *astronauts*. In the USSR, they were known as **cosmonauts**.

DOGS IN SPACE

Laika may have been the bravest dog in the world—or the solar system. She was the first living creature to orbit Earth. The Soviets launched her in 1957. But she died during the trip. The first dogs to orbit Earth and return safely were Strelka and Belka. They were sent into space in 1960 and parachuted back.

FIRST HUMAN IN SPACE

What did the first man in space feel 10 seconds before launch time? Was he terrified? No human had ever been in space. Did he wonder if he would die?

Yuri Gagarin was the first human in space. The Soviets successfully launched him into space in the *Vostok 1* capsule on April 12, 1961. After orbiting once, he was ejected from the craft and parachuted back to Earth. He spent 108 minutes in space.

Rats, monkeys, frogs, spiders, newts, and bees have all been sent into space!

COSMONAUTS

What does it take to be a cosmonaut? The first male cosmonauts were military pilots. Valentina Tereshkova was the first woman in space. Before that, she was a factory worker. But she had a taste for adventure. That is an important quality for those blasting into space. In the USSR, thousands of people applied to become the first person in space. Twenty were chosen for testing. They were tested physically and mentally. Above all, they needed to stay calm in stressful situations. Yuri Gagarin was chosen because he stayed calm through all the tests.

cosmonauts Gagarin and Tereshkova

SPACE FASHION

Astronauts wear suits that protect them from the extreme temperatures of space. The suits have life-support systems built in and protect against space dust.

Noril'sk

RUSSIA

Yakutsk

Krasnoyarsk

Irkutsk

JUST IN CASE

Russia, formerly part of the USSR, is a large country with many wilderness areas. In these places there are wolves, bears, and other animals. Cosmonauts were each given a hunting knife to take with them—just in case the capsule landed somewhere with dangerous creatures!

Urumqi

MON

CHINA

THE RIGHT STUFF

In the United States, the first seven astronauts were military pilots. Before going into space, their job was to test new planes. They had to go through a lot of training and testing. No one was sure what space might be like. NASA wanted the astronauts to be ready for anything. The astronauts needed to be able to fly complicated machines. They had to be able to stay calm in a crisis. Astronauts were tested for physical fitness. They would be asked to follow difficult orders.

the original seven NASA astronauts

Astronaut Sunita Williams speaks with reporters during a press conference.

HERO TRAINING

Astronauts don't just fly spacecrafts. They are national heroes. They must learn how to answer questions from reporters. The government does not want them to say anything that might make the space program look bad.

WHAT EVER HAPPENED TO?

Many astronauts had impressive careers after they returned from space. John Glenn, the first American to orbit Earth, became a US senator. A dozen years after his 1969 flight to the moon, Alan Bean became an artist. Many astronauts stayed with the space program to teach new crews. Others became business leaders or teachers.

DO YOU HAVE WHAT IT TAKES?

Less than 1,000 people have been chosen to be astronauts. Astronauts must have the right skills and personality for the job. Use this quiz to find out if you've got what it takes. Give yourself a point every time you answer *yes* to the questions below. If you score three or better, then you're on your way to becoming an astronaut! If not, don't worry! You have plenty of time to train.

Start here!

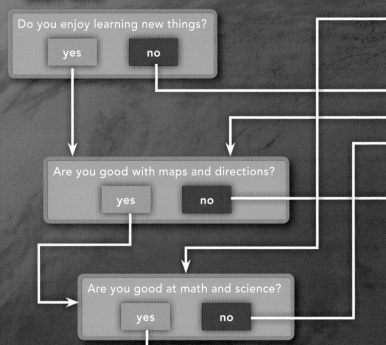

Do you enjoy learning new things?
yes   no

Are you good with maps and directions?
yes   no

Are you good at math and science?
yes   no

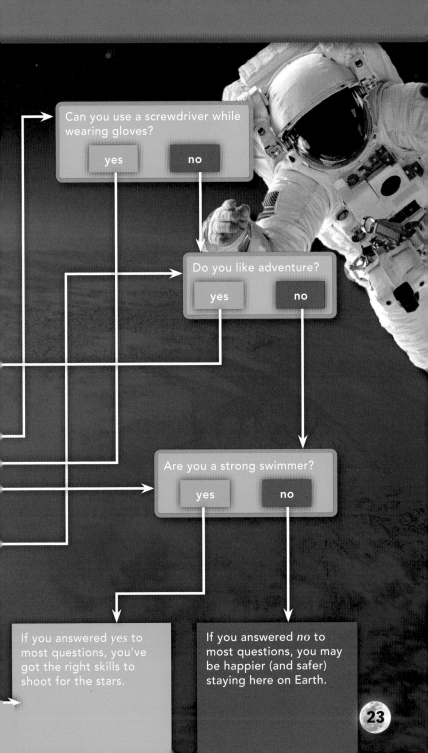

Can you use a screwdriver while wearing gloves?

yes   no

Do you like adventure?

yes   no

Are you a strong swimmer?

yes   no

If you answered *yes* to most questions, you've got the right skills to shoot for the stars.

If you answered *no* to most questions, you may be happier (and safer) staying here on Earth.

GREAT MINDS

The space programs needed people with a variety of skills. Teams of engineers designed the spacecrafts. Wernher Von Braun led the team in the United States. He had designed rockets for Germany during World War II. But his real love was exploring space. He led the United States' space program until 1970. In the USSR, the chief designer was Sergei Koroloyov. He was a brilliant engineer. He worked with rockets from the 1930s until he died in 1966.

MISHIN DIARIES

The Soviet space program was kept secret. But one man kept a diary that recorded his work. Vasily Mishin was one of Koroloyov's deputies. His diary provides insights about the people who worked on the project and lets us learn their secrets many years later.

Mishin (left) with other Soviet scientists

VON BRAUN AND DISNEY

Wernher Von Braun and Walt Disney worked together on three educational movies about space. Von Braun wanted to get the public excited about space exploration. He thought Disney could help.

The USSR kept Sergei Koroloyov's identity a secret until his death.

DISASTERS

The early space programs were dangerous. The teams were pushing themselves. They wanted to be the first at something no one had tried before. Both countries had many setbacks and heart-wrenching losses. But they kept working toward their goals. The Soviets hoped their *N1 rocket* would take people to the moon. But on July 3, 1969, the rocket exploded on the launch pad. This was one of the largest explosions in history. It destroyed the launch pad. After this loss, the United States team was able to beat the Soviets to the moon.

January 27, 1967
The Apollo 1 crew died when a fire swept through their space capsule. They were rehearsing launch procedures.

March 23, 1961
Valentin Bondarenko was killed in a fire while training.

Becoming an astronaut is dangerous. Why do you think so many people still apply for the job?

April 24, 1967
Vladimir Komarov was killed when the parachute on his space capsule didn't open on reentry into Earth's atmosphere.

March 27, 1968
Yuri Gagarin, the first man in space, was killed in a training crash.

June 29, 1971
The *Soyuz 11* crew died when a valve on their craft opened as they came back to Earth. All the oxygen escaped into space, and they suffocated.

A DANGEROUS JOB

It is rare, but people still die on space missions. On January 28, 1986, the **space shuttle** *Challenger* exploded. All seven astronauts on board were killed. On February 1, 2003, there was another tragedy. The shuttle *Columbia* broke apart. Again, the entire crew was killed.

It is always a risk to fly into space, so why do people do it? Some astronauts complete the training to earn respect. Others want to learn about space. They want to help us find out what is out there. Each person has his or her own personal reasons. And each reason is in some way noble.

BASSETT, CHARLES A. II
BELYAYEV, PAVEL I.
CHAFFEE, ROGER B.
DOBROVOLSKY, GEORGI T.
FREEMAN, THEODORE C.
GAGARIN, YURI A.
GIVENS, EDWARD G., Jr.
GRISSOM, VIRGIL I.
KOMAROV, VLADIMIR M.
PATSAYEV, VIKTOR I.
SEE, ELLIOT M., Jr.
VOLKOV, VLADISLAV N.
WHITE, EDWARD H. II
WILLIAMS, CLIFTON C., Jr.

MOON MEMORIES

On their visit to the moon, the Apollo 15 crew left a small memorial to astronauts and cosmonauts who had lost their lives.

TEACHER IN SPACE

Christa McAuliffe was one of the crew members on *Challenger*. She was going to be the first teacher in space. NASA chose her to get children and teachers more interested in space exploration.

APOLLO 13

Apollo 13 was supposed to go to the moon. But it never made it. An oxygen tank exploded in space. "Houston, we've had a problem," astronaut John Swigert reported calmly. It was a disaster. But the astronauts worked with people back home. They stayed focused on fixing the problem, and the entire crew made it back safely. This is an example of why NASA looks for people who can work well in a crisis.

Setting foot on the moon changed the way humans see Earth. From the ground, our planet appears large. But from space, Earth looks like a big, blue marble. And marbles—even big ones—are not that big compared to everything else. Seeing Earth from far away had a strong effect on astronauts. Looking at Earth from space, they felt connected to the universe in a way they had never felt on Earth. They saw how small and precious our planet is. This understanding of Earth is called the **overview effect**. NASA psychologists used the phrase **space euphoria** (yoo-FAWR-ee-uh) to describe it.

a footprint left on the moon by an astronaut

"The Earth reminded us of a Christmas tree ornament hanging in the blackness of space. As we got farther and farther away it diminished in size. Finally it shrank to the size of a marble, the most beautiful marble you can imagine. That beautiful, warm, living object looked so fragile, so delicate, that if you touched it with a finger it would crumble and fall apart. Seeing this has to change a man...."

—James Irwin, astronaut

EARTHRISE

The astronauts on Apollo 8 were the first to orbit around the moon. Each had seen many sunrises on Earth. But in space, they saw something new. They saw an **earthrise**. An earthrise is when Earth becomes visible over the horizon of the moon.

BEING THERE

Many of the planned space missions of the future will use robots instead of people. Why do you think robots are preferred over humans for future space travel? Do you think we lose something if humans don't make the trip?

a robonaut built to help humans explore space

Jim Lovell, William Anders, and Frank Borman of the Apollo 8 crew (left to right)

EARTHRISE, THE PICTURE

Earthrise is the name of a famous photograph of Earth rising over the moon. The following conversation took place between astronauts Frank Borman and William Anders just before the picture was taken. Back then, there was no such thing as a digital camera. Cameras used rolls of film.

Borman: Look at that picture over there! Here's the Earth coming up. Wow, is that pretty.

Anders: Hey, don't take that, it's not scheduled.

Borman: (laughing) You got a color film, Jim?

Anders: Hand me that roll of color quick, will you...

THE EAGLE HAS LANDED

On July 16, 1969, Neil Armstrong, Buzz Aldrin, and Michael Collins sat strapped in *Saturn V*. They were about to make history. This was the Apollo 11 space mission, and their rocket would take them to the moon.

Four days later, Aldrin and Armstrong climbed into the Eagle lunar **module**. They headed to a spot on the moon known as the Sea of Tranquility. They radioed, "Houston, Tranquility Base here. The Eagle has landed." Back on Earth, the crew roared with joy. They had made it to the moon!

CUTTING IT CLOSE

There were only 30 seconds of fuel left in the Eagle when Armstrong landed on the moon. If it had taken him a few seconds more to land, they would have had to abort the moon landing.

Neil Armstrong

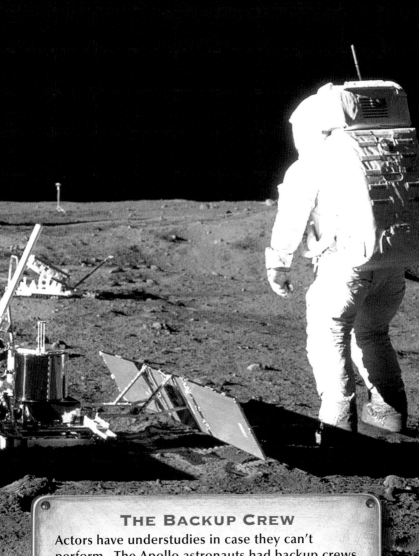

THE BACKUP CREW

Actors have understudies in case they can't perform. The Apollo astronauts had backup crews for the same reason. These astronauts had to train just like the main crew. They had to be ready to take over if they were needed. They worked just as hard as the main crew, but none of the backups ever made it to the moon that summer.

PERFECT TIMING

Getting to the moon was no easy task. Every part of the journey was planned and plotted ahead of time. Astronauts knew what to expect each step of the way. And the timing had to be just right. Bad timing could lead to a **catastrophic** mistake. Every piece of equipment and every person had to be in the right place at the right time. If they made a mistake, they might not have reached their destination. And they wouldn't have had enough fuel to get back.

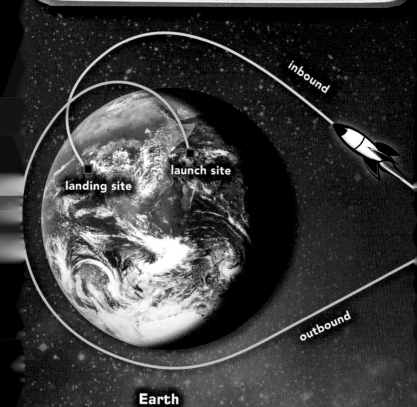

inbound

launch site

landing site

outbound

Earth

- Why are parts of Earth and the moon in shadow?

- What is the difference between the yellow and the blue lines?

- Why might the launch location and touchdown location on Earth be different?

launch site

landing site

the moon

IN THE DRIVER'S SEAT

The spacecraft that went to the moon didn't come back in one piece. Most of the spacecraft stayed in space. It had been built in sections. Each section played an important role in the mission. Once it was used, that part of the spacecraft wasn't needed. The only part to return with the astronauts was the small command module.

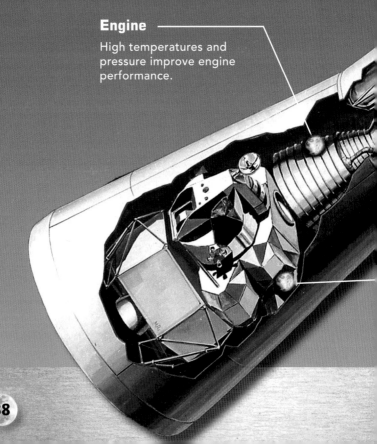

Engine

High temperatures and pressure improve engine performance.

Anatomy of a Moon Rocket

Launch Escape System

In case of an emergency, this top-mounted rocket allows the crew to escape from the rest of the rocket quickly.

Command Module

The astronauts lived in the command module. This was the section that returned them to Earth.

Service Module

The service module had the astronauts' food, fuel, oxygen, and supplies. It stayed with the command module until it was no longer needed. Then, it burned up in the atmosphere. The command and service modules orbited the moon but did not go to the surface.

Lunar Module

The lunar module was designed to land on the moon. It had two parts. The landing stage stayed on the moon after the astronauts left. The upper stage flew back to the rest of the ship.

MOONWALK

On July 20, 1969, Neil Armstrong became the first person to step onto the moon. On Earth, 500 million people watched. The astronauts were on television. It was thrilling! Armstrong announced, "That's one small step for man, one giant leap for mankind." Between 1969 and 1972, there were six successful moon missions. In all, 12 people have walked on the moon.

WATCHING FROM HOME

Imagine sitting in your living room with your family watching Neil Armstrong step out onto the moon's surface for the first time. How would you feel? Many people were inspired. They were amazed at what humans had accomplished. And they began to dream about what might come next.

MOON PLAQUE

The Apollo 11 crew left a plaque at their landing site. It reads:

HERE MEN FROM THE PLANET EARTH
FIRST SET FOOT UPON THE MOON
JULY A.D. 1969
WE CAME IN PEACE FOR ALL MANKIND

THE MAN IN THE MOON

Most cultures have stories that explain the way the moon looks. Some thought the dark spots were oceans on the moon. Others thought the moon looked like a face. People from around the world have said they see the outline of a woman knitting, a crab, and a man reading under a tree. In Asia, they often say there is a rabbit living on the moon. Do you see pictures in the moon?

The oldest parts of the moon are the light-color areas. They formed from cooling **magma**.

The light-color areas have craters and basins.

What do you see in the moon?

a rabbit?

a crab?

a woman knitting?

The dark areas are a type of volcanic rock called *basalt*.

Craters were formed by large objects crashing into the moon's surface.

EXPLORING THE MOON

Throughout history, people have explored new lands. They had no idea what they would find. But they wanted to know more about these places. It's the same for astronauts, perhaps the greatest explorers in history. They had no idea what they would find in space. But they knew they wanted to learn as much about it as possible.

The moon is covered with leftover experiments. Discarded equipment from Earth still remains. Flags, lunar modules, and probes lie there. Some astronauts left behind **mementos**. One of the most useful tools that astronauts left on the moon was a laser reflector. Scientists on Earth can shine a laser at the reflector. Then, they measure how long it takes for the light to bounce back. Using the reflector, they have learned the moon is moving away from Earth. It moves slowly at a rate of about 1.5 inches each year.

GENERAL DECLARATION

(Outward/Inward)

AGRICULTURE, CUSTOMS, IMMIGRATION, AND PUBLIC HEALTH

NATIONAL AERONAUTICS AND SPACE ADMINISTRATION

Owner or Operator ___ U.S.A. Flight No. APOLLO 11 Date JULY 24, 196_

Marks of Nationality and Registration ___ MOON Arrival at ___ HONOLULU, HAWAII

Departure from ___

FLIGHT ROUTING

("Place" Column always to list origin, every en-route stop and destination)

PLACE	TOTAL NUMBER OF CREW	NUMBER OF PASSENGERS ON THIS STAGE
CAPE KENNEDY	COMMANDER NEIL A. ARMSTRONG	
MOON	COLONEL EDWIN E. ALDRIN, JR.	
JULY 24, 1969 HONOLULU	LT. COLONEL MICHAEL COLLINS	

Departure Place:
Embarking
Through on same flight

Arrival Place:
Disembarking
Through on same flight

Declaration of Health

Persons on board known to be suffering from illness other than airsickness or the effects of accidents, as well as those cases of illness disembarked during the flight: NONE

Any other condition on board which may lead to the spread of disease:
TO BE DETERMINED

CLEARING CUSTOMS

When the Apollo 11 astronauts returned to the United States they signed **customs** documents, describing what they had brought back from the moon. The form says their cargo was "moon rock and moon dust samples" and is signed by all three astronauts.

44

A LASTING IMPRESSION

Apollo 16 astronaut Charles Duke left a photo of his family and a medal in a plastic bag on the surface of the moon. The astronauts also took samples of moon rocks and soil. They brought them back for scientists to study.

WHAT'S NEXT?

The first trips to the moon were only the beginning. The universe is vast. There is so much to learn and explore. There was never any problem thinking of new things to try. The only problem was figuring out which things to try next.

TRAFFIC JAM

Right now, there are about 8,000 satellites orbiting Earth. Most of those are "dead" satellites or debris. But about 560 of them are **operational**.

Russian satellite GLONASS

THE AGE OF SATELLITES

Sputnik 1 kicked off the space race. But it was only the first of thousands of satellites to be launched into orbit around Earth. Today, satellites let us make phone calls to most places on the planet. They keep track of the weather and do research. They help people on Earth navigate in cars, planes, and ships.

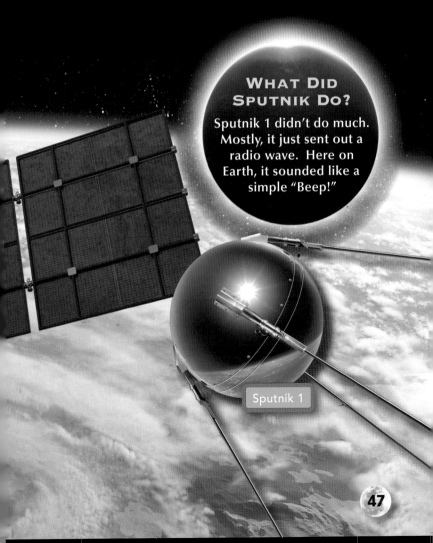

WHAT DID SPUTNIK DO?

Sputnik 1 didn't do much. Mostly, it just sent out a radio wave. Here on Earth, it sounded like a simple "Beep!"

Sputnik 1

SPACE SHUTTLES

In movies, people often take off and land on planets, using the same ship. When the space shuttle *Columbia* launched on April 12, 1981, science fiction became science fact. Space shuttles could go in to space and come back again. Before that, every mission required a different spacecraft. Shuttles were used to launch satellites. They carried pieces into space to create a **space station**. And they helped scientists do a lot of research.

THE LIFE OF SPACE SHUTTLE *ATLANTIS*

Number of Missions: 33

Time Spent in Space:
306 days: 14 hours: 12 minutes: 43 seconds

 First Flight:
October 3, 1985

 Last Flight:
July 8, 2011

Each shuttle was designed to be used about 100 times.

ALL GOOD THINGS COME TO AN END

After 30 years, the space shuttle program ended. The final mission was flown by shuttle *Atlantis* in July 2011.

SPACE STATIONS

Space stations are large satellites. They allow astronauts to live and work in space for long periods of time. This lets scientists do experiments that take more time. The astronauts even perform tests on themselves. Doctors study their **vital signs** to see how humans survive in space. Space stations are usually sent up into space in pieces. Then, the pieces are attached. Many countries work together in the space stations that orbit Earth.

American and Russian scientists work together on the International Space Station (ISS).

Every 90 minutes, the International Space Station circles Earth.

COME TOGETHER

The ISS is the ninth space station to be built. Astronauts and cosmonauts from 15 nations have lived on the ISS.

INSIDE THE ISS

The International Space Station is the largest spacecraft ever built. It is also the most expensive. NASA coordinated with countries around the world to build it. Up to six scientists can live on it full-time. To date, it has been occupied by at least 1 human for the last 11 years.

SPACE TOILETS

In space, even the basics need to be thought through. People can't just sit on a toilet. There is no gravity, so they (and their waste!) would float away. Toilets on the space station have a bar that keeps astronauts strapped down. And they use suction to make sure everything goes where it needs to go!

It took more than 15 countries working together to build the space station. Check out the diagram below to see when and where each piece was built.

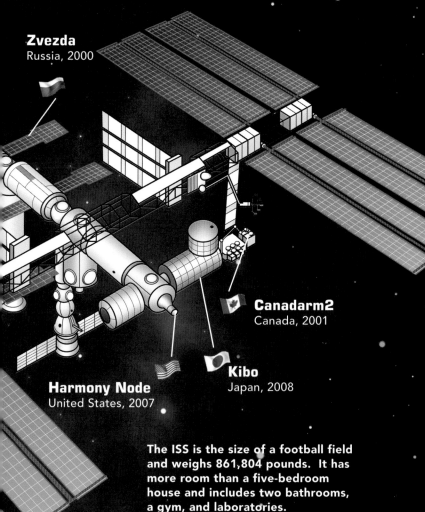

Zvezda
Russia, 2000

Canadarm2
Canada, 2001

Kibo
Japan, 2008

Harmony Node
United States, 2007

The ISS is the size of a football field and weighs 861,804 pounds. It has more room than a five-bedroom house and includes two bathrooms, a gym, and laboratories.

SPECTACULAR STATIONS

The first space station was the Soviet Union's Salyut 1. It was launched in 1971. The first American space station was Skylab. It was also the largest craft ever put into orbit. But Skylab was damaged in its launch, so it was only used for three missions. In 1986, the Russians launched Mir. It was used until 2001. China launched its first space station in September 2011. The Tiangong 1 will be the first of several sections. When all the pieces are in place, multiple spaceships will be able to dock at the same time.

EYES IN THE SKY

Scientists use space stations to study our planet in ways that aren't possible anywhere else.

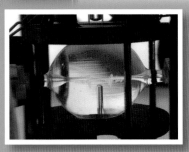

Growing special crystals in zero gravity may lead to faster computers or new ways to fight diseases.

Telescopes record changes in Earth's weather and study the big picture.

Space stations are great places to test how to grow food for future space explorers.

Many studies observe how humans deal with being alone in a small place for long periods of time.

A GIANT LEAP

The 20th century took humankind "one giant leap" forward in space exploration. The space race challenged us to work hard, learn more, and get to the moon no matter what. Sacrifices were made, human and animal lives were lost, but our vision of understanding and exploring space stayed true. Space exploration in the 20th century may have started off as the cutthroat space race. But by the end, nations from around the world learned to work together. Our history in space is brief, but it's marked with amazing firsts. What will we accomplish next? Only time will tell!

May 25, 1961

President Kennedy asks the United States to land a man on the moon within the decade.

April 12, 1961

Yuri Gagarin becomes the first man in space.

October 4, 1957

Soviets launch Sputnik 1, Earth's first artificial satellite.

July 20, 1969

The lunar module Eagle lands on the moon.

July 21, 1969

Neil Armstrong becomes the first human to set foot on the moon.

June 16, 1963

Valentina Tereshkova becomes the first woman in space.

April 19, 1971

The USSR launches Salyut 1, the world's first space station.

April 12, 1981

Columbia, the first reusable shuttle lands safely.

GLOSSARY

assassinated—murdered a government official or other
  public figure

astronauts—space travelers from the United States, also
  a general word for space travelers

catastrophic—disastrous

Cold War—a time period between 1945 and 1991 when
  the USSR and the United States were enemies but not
  openly fighting each other

cosmonauts—space travelers from the USSR or Russia

customs—the government agency or procedures for
  collecting fees charged for bringing goods into or out
  of a country

earthrise—the view of Earth becoming visible over the
  horizon of the moon

magma—a hot fluid beneath or within a planet or moon's
  crust

mementos—objects kept as reminders of past events

missiles—objects that are thrown, shot, or launched to hit
  something at a distance

module—a complete piece that is part of a bigger
  structure

operational—able to function

overview effect—the change that happened in people's
  attitudes when they were able to see Earth from space
  for the first time

rockets—spacecrafts that are powered by a rocket engine
  with gases that are released from burning fuel

satellite—an object that orbits Earth

Soviet Union—a country that existed across Europe and Asia from 1917 to 1991; also known as the USSR

space euphoria—a feeling of happiness and connection to the Earth and its people caused by seeing Earth from outer space

space race—the competition to be the first country to achieve goals in space exploration

space station—a large satellite where scientists live for months at a time

space shuttle—a kind of spacecraft that can return to Earth and be reused

Union of Soviet Socialist Republics (USSR)—a former group of 15 republics that spanned Europe and Asia, all of which are now separate countries

vital signs—the pulse rate, body temperature, number of breaths taken per minute, and blood pressure of a person

INDEX

Aldrin, Buzz, 34
Anders, William, 33
Apollo 1, 26
Apollo 8, 32–33
Apollo 11, 34, 41, 44
Apollo 13, 29
Apollo 15, 28
Apollo 16, 45
Apollo program, 12–13
Armstrong, Neil, 34, 40, 57
astronauts, 4–5, 8, 14–16,
    19–22, 27–33, 35–36,
    38–40, 44–45, 50–52
Atlantis, 48–49
Bean, Alan, 21
Belka, 16
Bondarenko, Valentin, 26
Borman, Frank, 33
Canada, 53
Canadarm2, 53
Challenger, 28–29
China, 54
Cold War, 6, 8–9
Collins, Michael, 34
Columbia, 28, 48, 57
command module, 38–39
cosmonauts, 16, 18–19, 28,
    51
Disney, Walt, 25

Duke, Charles, 45
Eagle lunar module, 34, 57
Earth, 4, 6, 10–12, 16–17,
    21, 23, 27, 30–34,
    36–37, 39–41, 44,
    46–47, 50–51, 54, 56
earthrise, 32–33
Eisenhower, Dwight D., 9
Explorer 1, 10
Florida, 14
Gagarin, Yuri, 10, 17–18,
    27, 56
Germany, 24
Glenn, John, 21
GLONASS, 46
Greek, 13
Harmony Node, 53
International Space Station
    (ISS), 50–53
Irwin, James, 31
Japan, 53
Kennedy Space Center, 14
Kennedy, John F., 12, 14,
    56
Kibo, 53
Komarov, Vladimir, 27
Koroloyov, Sergei, 24–25
laboratories, 53
Laika, 10, 16

launch escape system, 39
Leonov, Alexei, 11
Lovell, Jim, 33
lunar module, 39, 44, 57
McAuliffe, Christa, 29
Mir, 54
Mishin, Vasily, 24
missiles, 8–9
modules, 39, 44
N1 rocket, 26
National Aeronautics and
    Space Administration
    (NASA), 5, 14, 20,
    29–30, 52
overview effect, 30
probes, 44
rocket garden, 14
rockets, 6, 8, 14, 24, 26,
    34, 39
Russia, 19, 53
Russians, 54
Salyut 1, 54, 57
satellite, 4, 7–8, 10, 46–48,
    50, 56
Saturn V, 34
scientists, 4, 6, 10, 12, 24,
    44–45, 48, 50, 52, 54
Sea of Tranquility, 34
service module, 39

Skylab, 54
Soviet Union, 4, 12, 54
Soviets, 6–7, 9–10, 12,
    16–17, 24, 26, 56
Soyuz 11, 27
space euphoria, 30
space race, 5–6, 10, 47, 56
space stations, 48, 50–55,
    57
space toilets, 52
Sputnik 1, 7, 10–11, 47, 56
Strelka, 16
Swigert, John, 29
Tereshkova, Valentina, 11,
    18, 57
Tiangong 1, 54
United States, 4, 6, 8, 10,
    12, 16, 20, 24, 26, 44,
    53, 56
USSR, 6–8, 16, 18–19,
    24–25, 57
Von Braun, Wernher, 24–25
Vostok 1, 17
Williams, Sunita, 21
World War II, 6, 24
Zvezda, 53

BIBLIOGRAPHY

Adamson, Thomas K., *The First Moon Landing.* **Capstone Press, 2007.**

This graphic novel tells the story of the Apollo 11 mission. It includes a real astronaut-to-mission control conversation, a map of moon landings, and fun illustrations.

Aldrin, Buzz. *Reaching for the Moon.* **Perfection Learning, 2008.**

Astronaut Buzz Aldrin tells the story of his historic journey to the moon. His journey started before he was an astronaut—it began when he was a young child. Learn more about Aldrin, his dreams, and how they came true.

Starke, John. *High Definition 3D Space.* **Sterling, 2009.**

Get ready to blast off into space! You will fly the space shuttle, land on the moon, visit a space station, and more. With your 3-D glasses, you'll experience deep space like never before! Don't forget to answer the debriefing questions after your mission.

Wolfe, Hillary. *Blast Off to Space Camp.* **Teacher Created Materials, 2011.**

Find out if you have what it takes to be an astronaut. Check out what it's like to train for a space mission, wear a flight suit, and live in zero gravity as you learn about NASA's world-famous space camp.

MORE TO EXPLORE

We Choose the Moon

http://www.wechoosethemoon.org

Click *Launch* to hear real recordings from mission control as you see Apollo 11 take off. Each leg of the journey has pictures, videos, and audio from this historic launch.

Walking on the Moon

http://www.smithsonianeducation.org/idealabs/walking_on_the_moon /index.html

What did it take to put people on the moon? What were the dangers? Who were the astronauts that first stepped onto the moon? All these questions and more will be answered as you relive the mission.

Apollo 11

http://www.nasa.gov/externalflash/apollo11_landing

This video features the first manned lunar module to land on the moon. You will hear authentic audio from the mission throughout the video. You can also watch the footage from Apollo 11's launch and view a 360° view of the surface of the landing site while listening to the transcript of the account.

Facts About the Moon

http://www.woodlands-junior.kent.sch.uk/time/moon/facts.htm

Learn more about Earth's moon. From its effect on the tides to the phases of the moon, this site has lots of information. You will also find tips for watching the moon as it goes through its different phases.

Stephanie Paris grew up in California. She received a degree in psychology from UC Santa Cruz and a teaching credential from CSU San Jose. She has been an elementary classroom teacher, an elementary school computer and technology teacher, a home-schooling mother, an educational activist, an educational author, a web designer, a blogger, and a Girl Scout leader. Ms. Paris currently lives with her husband and two children in Germany where she enjoys moon watching.